THERE IS A GOD
THERE IS NO GOD

D1397595

JOHN KIRVAN

author of *God Hunger*

THERE IS A GOD
THERE IS NO GOD

A Companion
for the Journey of
Unknowing

SORIN BOOKS   Notre Dame, Indiana

For this work, unless otherwise noted, the text of *The Cloud of Unknowing* has been taken from *Where Only Love Can Go: A Journey of the Soul Into the Cloud of Unknowing* by John Kirvan (Notre Dame, IN: Ave Maria Press), Copyright © 1996 by Quest Associates. It is a text that has been freely adapted into modern English, rearranged and paraphrased to meet the needs of a meditation format.

© 2003 by Quest Associates

www.sorinbooks.com

International Standard Book Number: 1-893732-69-X

Cover design by Eric Walljasper

Text design by Katherine Robinson Coleman

Printed and bound in the United States of America.

Library of Congress Cataloging-in-Publication Data

Kirvan, John J.

   There is a God, there is no God: a companion for the journey of unknowing / John Kirvan.

    p. cm.

   ISBN 1-893732-69-X (pbk.)

   1. Spiritual life--Christianity. 2. Cloud of unknowing. 3. Desire for God. I. Title.

  BV4501.3.K57 2003

  248.4--dc21

                              2003007143

As always for F.B.

But in a special way this book is

dedicated to all those

who must seek and find God

where he is not supposed to be.

Acknowledgments

Let me acknowledge
the work of three persons
who made this book possible—
Jon Pilon, Ken McGuire, C.S.P.,
and Robert Hamma for understanding
what I am trying to say.
You helped me find the right words,
even when I was tongue-tied.

Contents

PART ONE
THERE COMES A TIME

There comes a moment
when there arises in your soul
a movement that you are
at a loss to describe.

It moves you to desire
you know not what,
only that it is beyond your imagining.

It is God at work within you.

—The Cloud of Unknowing

There comes a moment when it is all but impossible to ignore God's persistent knocking at the doorways of our soul, when it is impossible to ignore his repeated invitations to come closer. To embrace the unknowable. To cast our lot with a God we cannot pretend to know, may never know. To surrender completely.

As much as I—as much as we—might try to fend off this moment, it happens. God happens.

We come to know and accept that just to hear the name of God is to have sowed in our soul the seeds of a hunger, of a discontent that will not go away. Our desire to go beyond an ordinary, decent life becomes an imperative that grows deeper and more urgent with every passing day

However it is for others, I confess that I no longer want to spend my days only half-alive, with an unrelenting God-hunger at the core of my being, my heart demanding that I respond some-how, someway. I am no longer content to live a life stitched together with routine gestures, with vacuous "maybes," with the convenience of "not here, not yet."

I no longer want to spend my life clinging to what I have. To what I know. It has never been enough. Even when I have wanted it to be. Even when God has seemed more a tyrant than a lover.

Even when I have wanted more than anything else to shake loose of her hold on my life.

There comes a moment when attention must be paid. A time to look, to listen, to stop running, a time to choose, a time to act, a time to forsake my safety zones, a time for letting down my defenses. A time for letting go.

A time to surrender my need to know, to understand.

A time to embrace mystery as my native land.

And silence as my native tongue

A time that may be for others a clear, defined moment.

But for me—a lingering subtle presence that has stolen quietly, almost imperceptibly into my consciousness.

I may try to deny it.

But it won't go away.

PART TWO
THE WAY OF UNKNOWING

Let God do his work.
Let him lead you, as he will.
He needs only your consent.

Be content not to see,
and put aside your need to know.

Accept that someone is moving
lovingly within you,
even if you do not yet recognize
that it is God at work.

—The Cloud of Unknowing

This insistent longing
cannot be fulfilled
by a deeper knowledge or understanding of God;
it is fulfilled only by "unknowing,"
only by love.

Sometime in the fourteenth century an anonymous young man for whom an ordinary, decent life was no longer enough turned for advice to an equally anonymous spiritual director.

Six centuries later we are still doing the same thing. Discontent with an ordinary, decent, life we are still turning to that anonymous wise man and getting the same advice.

In a remarkable document called *The Cloud of Unknowing*, he introduces us to a spiritual tradition that shatters the way most of us approach God.

Most of us grow up, and indeed grow old, quite sure that we know a great deal about God. Sometimes we take everything that the human race has discovered to be good, noble, beautiful, and true—everything indeed that we admire—and apply it in infinite terms to the God we believe in.

We have never seen that God, but we have seen his face in good, merciful, compassionate, generous human beings.

Some others may have seen a different face of God, a face of cruelty and indifference.

In his play *Suddenly Last Summer*, Tennessee Williams creates Sebastian, who, according to his mother, has seen the face of God. He saw it, she reports, in the Galapagos Islands, where he watched thousands of turtles hatch on the beach only to see them eaten by the birds before they could reach the ocean.

God is all of this for some of us—writ not just large, but infinitely vast.

We see what we see, good and bad, and we call it God.

Exhilarating or painful, this is our usual way of coming to "know" God.

But there is another way, the way of *The Cloud of Unknowing*, that is just as deeply rooted in Western spiritual tradition, though more deeply employed by the great mystics than by the rest of us. It is the "negative" way. This tradition embraces a God who totally escapes the power of our minds and our imaginations, the best efforts of our language. He is—she is—neither the avuncular old man nor the cruel master of his helpless creatures.

If we insist on thinking and talking about God—which we must—the most we can expect from our best efforts is to say what God is not. He—she—is utterly different, utterly other than anything we can experience or name.

We approach God, therefore, not by pushing the envelope of our rational efforts as far as it will go, but by accepting the ultimate limitations of our mind, by coming to understand that our journey is to a place where only love can go. We have a power to know and a power to love. When it comes to God, it is the latter that matters, that alone is possible.

This is the *via negativa*, the way of unknowing.

"We can never, through our reason alone, arrive at the knowledge of uncreated being, of what God alone is," the author of *The Cloud* reminds us. "But even in our inability, in our failure, we can indeed know God. As St. Denis said: 'the truly divine knowledge of God is that which is known by unknowing.'"

This is not a word game. It is love, not knowledge, that pierces the darkness, that overcomes the distance. We are invited here and now to begin the unending life of heaven, the only approach to God that death will not make superfluous.

We beginners on the spiritual path—apprentices, as the author calls us—may never be called to the demanding heights of contemplation. But this does not mean that time spent with *The Cloud of Unknowing* is an act of spiritual dilettantism. With all its talk of darkness, it sheds enormous light on the path of even the simplest seeker after God. Nothing illumines a path more than a sense of where it is leading. The author, obviously faced with similar criticism centuries ago, replied that even the simplest of us can find our way into real union with God in a simple, perfect love.

From the beginning of our quest and at every step, it is important to understand that the object, the goal of our faith and love, is God and God alone, not any of the thousand things we are tempted to substitute. The words are never the reality. *The Cloud of Unknowing* never lets us forget this.

In the very beginning of his work, the wise teacher instructs his readers that this is a journey that will make deep and insistent demands. It requires serious attention. It is not for those who are tempted to "dip into" spirituality, to play around the edges of contemplation, presuming that the journey to God is a trip into warm fuzziness and uninterrupted serenity.

Be warned: it is a terrible thing to fall into the hands of the living God. But never to dream of

escaping our words to find the heart of God—
what a loss!

Just to hear the name of God is, after all, to
have sowed in our soul the seeds of a discontent
that will not go away—the seeds of a love that
alone can satisfy our soul.

> *On this path of unknowing*
> *we accept the unremitting change,*
> *the incompleteness,*
> *and the contradiction*
> *that characterize our times.*

The "modern" world and the prevailing spiritual tradition into which we were born promised us a controllable and predictable universe in which we would know who we were, what we could do, and what we could expect of life.

It was a world defined by science and its promise that there was nothing that could not ultimately be understood, nothing that in time we could not control.

It was an aggressive time, when we thought—presumed—the world would bend to our will. It would, we were confident, surrender to our need to know, to our need to make sense and our conviction that sense could be made.

Mysteries were just problems waiting to be solved. We were, after all, the ultimate problem solvers, and our ability to make sense would be our salvation.

But our world would not be confined to the categories and structures we had created. Our world constructed with certitude and of certainty was dying. A "postmodern" world beyond our power to control, a world without certitude, security, and predictability was in the making, was already in place.

History was—still is—busily deconstructing the world we understood, in which we were at home, whose language we spoke. Our points of reference, our stability, and our certainties are crumbling. The rules by which we lived and through which we sought to understand each other, our world and our God are changing and continue to change even when they are not being set aside as antiquated and irrelevant.

When Walter Truett Anderson wrote about the emergence of this new postmodern world, he called his book: *Reality Isn't What It Used To Be.* It isn't. It will never be the same again.

The emerging world is likened to that moment when Adam and Eve, intensely aware of their nakedness, were thrust out of the Garden of Eden to face life in an utterly changed world. But it is not just that we have moved into a changed world—that has happened many times in history—it is that we are confronted with a world whose defining characteristic is change. We change—therefore we are. We cope with change or we cease to be: we die a slow, spiritual death.

To cope and to grow with change is not a matter of adopting the controversial values of a postmodern philosophy, the matter of many an easy sermon. It is a matter of our being brought face to face with the fact that unremitting change is not only the context of our spiritual journey, it is its raw material. It is the spiritual air we are destined to breathe.

We are forever, with every step, leaving behind what we thought we knew to enter into the unknown, the unknowable.

This path calls us to embrace a spirituality
that is at home with mystery.

However reluctantly, we are forced to admit that we have inherited a spirituality cut from the same cloth as the "modern" world—a spirituality that presumes a knowable, controllable, and predictable existence. It comes, often as not, with a presumption and a promise that the spiritual world is timeless and unchanging, that in fact spirituality is our protection against change and time.

In that spiritual world we know—we think—what God is like and what God expects. Where God can be found and where he is not.

And when we go in search of God, we know who and what we are looking for. And where to look.

We are in for a surprise. Many surprises. With more to come.

We discover, often painfully, that our inherited spirituality is for the most part not prepared to deal with the world we found.

We come to know, if not accept, that if we are to exist and to grow spiritually we will have to meet the challenge of unrelenting change.

We know it, but we struggle to avoid it.

Our first instinct was and still is to ignore and deny the fact that Humpty Dumpty has fallen and to go on with life and our prayers as usual.

Our second reaction was and is to busy ourselves putting Humpty-Dumpty back together in a shattered world, in a world where not only has the great, universal Humpty-Dumpty fallen but so too have a thousand personal Humpty-Dumpties. We instinctively reach for safety nets, to cling to some form of spirituality that makes a point of change-lessness—giving us something to hold on to—a spirituality of shelter and rescue from the storm.

We can run, but we cannot hide from change.

We need a spirituality that can measure up to the changing world that is endlessly evolving around and within us, a world in which reality is not what it used to be. And never will be again.

We need to find and follow a spiritual way that is at home with mystery, a way that does not deny or flee the unknowable, but rather embraces it.

Our need is not new. Nor is the path that stretches out before us.

As early as the fourth century, when another world was collapsing, Gregory of Nyssa looked for a metaphor of the spiritual journey. He chose the life of Moses, whose journey began in light but ended in darkness. "The soul leaves behind all that can be grasped by sense or reason, and the only thing left for her contemplation is the invisible and the incompressible. And it is here that God is. . . ."

Twelve centuries later, in the wake of the Renaissance, the great mystic and spiritual master John of the Cross would tell the serious seeker that the higher we ascend the less we will understand because "the cloud is dark." Whoever knows this, he wrote:

> Remains always in unknowing
> Transcending all knowledge.

A century later Angelus of Silesius wrote that because the God we are seeking is untouched by time or space . . .

> The more we reach for him
> The more he will escape.

In our own nuclear age Thomas Merton has confessed:

> My Lord God, I have no idea where
> I am going.
> I do not see the road ahead of me.
> I cannot know for certain where
> it will end.

Perhaps, however, no one has put it more starkly and more powerfully than Simone Weil.

"There is a God. There is no God," she wrote. "I am quite sure," she explained, "there is a God in the sense that I am sure my love is no illusion. I am quite sure there is no God in the sense that I am sure there is nothing which resembles what I can conceive when I say the word."

> *Our destiny is to go deeper*
> *and deeper into the dark.*

In and for every generation of seekers who have sought to go beyond an ordinary and decent life there have been men and women who have discovered, followed, and shared a way of darkness, a way of unknowing, a way of change, a spiritual tradition that the scholars called "apophatic."

Among them no one has been a better teacher and guide than the nameless spiritual teacher who coined the phrase "the cloud of unknowing" seven centuries ago.

His spiritual vision of a life centered in unknowing may have been first spoken to a young contemplative monk in search of an even more dedicated life. But it resonates just as strongly with all of us who live in changing times, who desire a new fuller life beyond what we already know.

Like the young seeker we too want to know what it takes to move beyond an ordinary, decent life to a life immersed in and enriched by the mysterious omnipresence of God—what it takes to live with what we do not know, what we cannot know, what we will never know.

His wisdom still speaks to anyone who wishes to live with the inescapable truth that in the real world mystery is the core truth of our existence.

"We can never, through our reason alone," he wrote, "arrive at the knowledge of uncreated being, of what God alone is….We cannot measure God. We cannot see him. Smell him or taste him. God is no thing. We cannot locate him. He is not some place. God is nowhere."

"You cannot see God clearly," he wrote, "through the light of your reason."

We are destined, he told us, to live in the dark, to live without knowing—and not to be afraid of it.

Our spiritual destiny, we have come to understand, if not accept, is not to break through darkness to light, but to go deeper and deeper into the dark. Not to go from unknowing to knowing, but to move from a world where we think we know, to a world where we know that we do not know and where we celebrate our unknowing.

Our destiny, we must recognize and acknowledge, is in a rich darkness that rescues us from a comfortable idolatry, from a conviction that we can capture God within the limits of our mind and imagination.

However tempting it may be, we shall not have strange gods before the God we cannot know.

It is not an acknowledgment that comes easily. It is, in fact, scary country because we are compelled to abandon our reliance on even the dim, flickering light that so far has illumined our path.

It is hard for us because we like to know where we are and where we are going.

Instead we are confronted with the utterly mysterious—what we come to see and accept as the totally unknowable.

This is true for all of us. Even for us beginners.

What the author of *The Cloud of Unknowing* and the whole tradition of mystics of which he is a part add to this truth of our spiritual existence is to spell out the extraordinary spiritual possibilities and consequences of following a way of unknowing.

On that day so many centuries ago, when he met with the young monk, his advice was simple and timely. It still is.

"I am well aware," the wise older monk said to the young man, "that until now you have been living an ordinary and decent life.

"But now with his great grace God is kindling your desire for more and fastening to it a leash of longing.

"He is not going to let you off easily.

"You will no longer be content to live at a distance from God.

"It is time for you to look ahead and forget what is behind you, time to pay attention to what you still need, rather than to what you already have."

The longing we experience
is not for something quantifiable,
but for God.

Centuries after that meeting of the young seeker and the wise older monk we recognize the nameless young man as our brother in the Spirit.

We know that for us, as for the young man, there comes a time—now, perhaps?—when an ordinary, decent life is no longer enough. A time when we "get no satisfaction."

Sooner or later we reach that point.

Something happens to raise the expectations of our soul. No one, perhaps, has captured this moment more succinctly than the brilliant young movie director Eric Valle. When he was eighteen, he trekked across Syria and Afghanistan: "thirsty for life and looking for God."

"Afterwards," he said, "I could not go back into any little shoe box."

We recognize the truth of this image instantly. There comes a moment when our soul can no longer be boxed.

Our life, perhaps, is interrupted by some deep shattering pain. Age, perhaps, a midlife crisis of the spirit. Or the religion into which we were born and within which we have lived collapses all around us. Perhaps we catch a soul-expanding glimpse of a world beyond our imagining, beyond our comfort. We catch glimpses of another self that in some profound way we know is who we are called to be, the person we want to be, a self that is waiting to be born. It is a kind of spiritual midlife crisis. A midlife genesis.

Perhaps nothing more dramatic happens than a brush of our desire against the ordinariness of our days, but it is enough to open in our souls a spiritual discontent—a feeling that our life is meant to be more than it has been, that we are something less than whole.

Whatever has happened, in that moment God has kindled our desire for what the wise monk has called a life beyond ordinary decency.

It may be a new experience or an old one revisited. That's not important. What matters is that at this moment there is a hunger great enough to compel our surrender, a hunger for "more" that will not be denied.

Not more of the same. Not more prayers. Not more spiritual books. Not more meditation time. Not more exercises.

Not a quantifiable "more," not something that can be added to or added up. But a "more" that escapes our power to define. A "more" that matches the hunger of our soul, our hunger for

God, the hunger that gnaws at our spiritual complacency.

We know at the heart of our being that nothing less than what only God can give will ever be enough to fill the emptiness we feel. God has kindled in us an unquenchable desire for more.

To embrace this longing
is to be led along a path
unlike any we have ever traveled.

To that "more" God joins "a leash of longing."

We are invited to take the next step, knowing full well that to accept is to enter into the mystery of her pull on our whole being. It is to choose life beyond what we know, beyond what we have always known. It is to choose what we do not know, what we cannot know, not ever.

We are being told that the time has come to let go of everything with which we are comfortable— to consent to God's turning our life upside down, inside out, to have knowing replaced with unknowing, the familiar and the comfortable replaced with mystery and faith, security with hope, light with darkness, power with weakness, control with dependence.

This is more than we expected. Much more, perhaps.

It is a lot to ask of our soul. It is a lot that our soul asks of us.

But this much is certain: where we are coming from, where we are, is not where we want to be or where we want to stay.

We are no longer comfortable with a God who is just part of our history, a dependable presence. She exercises an all-but-irresistible undertow pulling us toward a world where we desire to be, but where nothing will ever be the same.

We are being led on a leash of longing unlike anything else we have ever known, unlike any other force we have ever felt at work in our soul.

I cannot speak for you, but I respond to this invitation—however imperative—half in desire, half in fear. Nothing, after all, will be left untouched. Nothing unchanged. Everything will be at risk. What I have will never again be enough.

But my soul tells me that the moment has come, as deep down I knew it would, to lower my protective barriers, to make an act of faith in a God that I will never see or understand. The moment has come to replace my need for certitude with a life lived in mystery, a willingness to go where ideas are no longer important, where force is useless, where control is out of the question.

The moment has come for my hope to take root in an incomprehensible God, a God no longer cut down to size before we take a chance on her—the risk of faith no longer minimized or delayed.

The moment has come to have my need— our need—for "more" met with more than I can imagine, and not at all what I might imagine.

God has kindled my desire for more, a life that goes beyond ordinary decency. My soul is being led on a divine leash of longing.

But it's not for the first time . . .

You, too, perhaps, have been here before. Perhaps frequently.

> *It is a path of "forgetting,"*
> *where we struggle*
> *to leave our idols and*
> *pretensions behind us.*

The desire for "more" that has been reignited in our soul is not easily satisfied.

The "more" we desire is one that lives up to our longing, to what C. S. Lewis calls "our lifelong nostalgia, our longing to be reunited with something in the universe from which we feel cut off, to be on the inside of some door which we have always seen from the outside."

There is nothing vacuous about this longing, nothing quantifiable about this "more."

The "more" for which we long is not, cannot be, an add-on, not a parallel existence—not mere reclothing of our soul, not a new vocabulary or a cause of the month. Nothing for which a membership card is required. Not a cosmetic. Not an accessorizing of our life, not adopting a new look, acting out, celebrating a new lifestyle. It is not role-playing. It is not something to be put on or taken off.

Nor is it a pocket library of familiar prayers and attitudes, handy when and should they be needed.

This may seem like an unnecessarily long litany of the obvious. But it gets to the core of the matter. We know that everything on this list is a ploy that at some moment in our life, certainly in my life, passed for the real thing, or at least for a moment appeared to be enough to satisfy our God-driven longing for more.

There have been, almost certainly still are, dozens, hundreds of pretenders to the throne— and the greatest of these is our own guilty secret. We have not yet given up the notion that we are God.

Our task—the one our wise teacher calls "forgetting"—is to dethrone all our false gods, above all else to overthrow our pretensions to divinity. And to do this without losing the mysterious reality of our own unique identity. Or the pull of the longing that floods our life.

There is no easy way to do this. Perhaps because so many of the great spiritual teachers left the city for the desert, left their homes for privileged silence and solitude and provided language for our spiritual journey, we frequently and easily fall into the trap of thinking that spirituality is bought at the price of ordinary life abandoned.

We start thinking about and acting as though there is something called "life" and something else called "spiritual life" as though they are two different worlds, two different lives, as often as not at warfare with each other. One is a world of common everyday experiences and responsibilities, the other a special life that you gain entrance to on the day you throw away your electric bill.

But we have only one life to live.

We may talk of radical spiritual change, of transforming our lives, but our family, whom we love, and the homeless, nameless family on a city street—none of them go away. Nor do the fidelity, support, generosity, and courage which we owe them. The light bill still has to be paid. The hungry still have to be fed.

It dawns on us, however slowly, however unnervingly that to overthrow our petty gods is to fundamentally redefine what it will mean for us to come fully alive, what it will mean to be fully human. We will have put an end to our idolatry. We will be not less human, but more fully human. Living not a new life, not some split life, but living to its full capacity the only life we have.

But there is more to it. To all of it.

There are some things that we can and must do as we topple our gods. There are some things that only God can do. The problem comes when we think it is all up to us.

Our life is transformed—not destroyed—at that moment when we let God do what only God can do. It has nothing to do with where we are or how we make sense of our lives. Certainly it is not confined to idyllic afternoons on mountain lakes. It can happen in our bed or while changing a diaper or depositing a paycheck—or in a monastery cell. That moment when we say and accept that we are not God, the guilty secret that so many of us hide and hide behind is penetrated.

From that moment on it is a matter of getting out of the way and letting God do what only he can do.

We need to listen again as the wise man talks to the young man, and to us.

A wall, a cloud of unknowing is rising before us.

Our longing will not go away. His leash will not loosen.

There is no timetable for this process;
transformation occurs on God's time.

It is in this moment that we begin to understand that our spiritual journey is not so much about possessing God—which cannot be done—as it is about leaving behind the possessions on which, until now, we have built our security. It is about leaving behind in a cloud of forgetting anything and everything that can stand between us and the God who awaits us in a cloud of unknowing.

It is a matter of forgetting, detaching, and disengaging from our ordinary, decent life, and consenting to a conversion of heart, to what the Greeks called a *metanoia*, or what we have come to call a transformation.

Our God is waiting for us to embrace the unknowable, to join the unknowing, to go where only love can go.

But it is a tricky and treacherous path.

One problem is that when we speak the dramatic language of transformation it can sound like an event rather than the process that it is. We are tempted to look for high melodrama, a clear-cut moment wrapped in the sensational and highlighted with special effects. But there is no "aha!" moment.

We carry with us images of Moses and Sinai's burning bush, of Paul thrown from his horse on the road to Damascus. There is the Buddha enlightened under the Bodhi Tree. There is Francis taking off his clothes, and walking naked into the consciousness (and conscience) of every generation since. We have heard of mystics whose body suddenly bleeds with the wounds of the crucifixion. There is talk of trances that carry the chosen out of their body. There is also Mr. Jones in a sweaty tent meeting proclaiming his salvation, and Mrs. Smith hitting the glory road, bathed in the full blaze of television lights.

All this drama can be very interesting, even invigorating, but it is basically misleading. It is, as frequently as not, the Promised Land of snake oil vendors, of the prophets of thirty-day miracle cures, of agents of ecstasy.

But flash is not to the point. It has, in fact, nothing to do with the experience of spiritual transformation. It never has. Looking for drama, or expecting it, is the best way to insure our taking wrong turns, being late for our meeting, ending up in the wrong place, or missing it entirely. The norm is—and always has been—the ordinary, the every-day, and the commonplace: moments when God's still small voice gets heard without ceremony, fanfare, or klieg lights, but with no less an effect on our life.

Mounting our expectations on the back of history's great conversions carries with it the seed of still another spiritual booby trap. Spiritual change, it could seem, is not only dramatic, but instantaneous. But transforming moments are hardly ever dramatic. They are certainly almost always the end product of a long, slow, often exasperating process that is frustratingly wedded to the commonplace.

One thing we can learn from these moments—and seldom do—is that transforming moments are not within our control. It's never a question of "your place or mine." It is always God's place. It is always God's timetable. She doesn't make appointments. She doesn't keep a daybook. Which means that there is no point in going around seeking some approved time and place where God will greet us according to a prearranged schedule.

We just have to take God as she is and where she is, unpredictable and unknowable. And though we use the language of search, it is not a question of our going anywhere, of seeking anywhere: it is a question of being found, a matter of surrender to a pursuing God.

Here's how Augustine put it: "You would not be searching if you had not already found."

What we understand to have been present all along reveals itself only very slowly and deliberately, wholly dependent on our letting its voice be heard (we would not be listening if we had not already heard), its presence felt.

Transformation, conversion, is not about bringing God into our lives. It is always about discovering and acknowledging the God who is already present.

We journey between two clouds:
again and again placing all that is false
in a cloud of forgetting
as we approach the illusive cloud of unknowing.

God does the transforming.

But there is something we can and must do.

Our role is to lower the noisy decibels of our soul and to break the spiritually obstructive habits of a lifetime, to enter into a cloud of forgetting, a cloud of disengagement with all that stands between us and an ever present God.

"Our task now," the wise man has written, "is the hard and unending one of putting behind us, of consigning to a Cloud of forgetting, all that

39

must be put aside if we are to approach Unknowing, if we are to love God and God alone."

"This is our task. Everything else belongs to God, and God alone. To do this even with the help of great grace requires hard labor on your part.

"But if you work hard, if you press on in the task of leaving behind all that stands between you and God, then God, I promise you, will not fail you.

"But he is waiting for you to do your part."

Our longing, our discontentment,
is an inescapable part of who we are.

There is no question that a part of me—a part of you, too, perhaps—will go on clinging to the hope that a spiritual transformation will bring with it contentment—a sense of satisfaction, of serenity, of monkish solitude, security, completion, and perfection. One more afternoon on a mountain lake. All those "spiritual" things.

We should know better. We probably, at the center of our soul, do.

Spirituality is not about contentment but about living with our discontent, living with a restless longing for something better, for something more, living between the cloud of forgetting and the cloud of unknowing.

Living a spiritual life is about dissatisfaction, about restlessness and hunger—about an ever-gnawing discontent with the distance that stretches between us and God.

It is about our no longer wanting to live with that distance, being willing to live with it nonetheless.

If we are lucky our discontent grows. As it should. As it must if we are to grow.

This discontent is not a passing emotion, not a momentary frustration, but an ongoing state of being. We are never quite where we want to be. We never run out of things that need to be forgotten, that need to be put behind us. We never reach so far into unknowing that we are content to say "far enough."

Our journey is driven not just by a longing for more, but by our acceptance that with every breath we come to understand more deeply that there will always be more, that we will always be hungry and never be satisfied, that our longing, our discontent is an inescapable part of who we are.

The spirituality of Unknowing is a spirituality of discontent, of desire, of restlessness, of longing for something better, for something more.

It is a kind of spirituality uniquely suited to our times.

A Canadian reviewer of new books about Thomas Merton recently made the point that spirituality in our times, of which Merton's spirituality is an archetypal example, is destined to be a spirituality of incompleteness and contradiction. "We will," he wrote, "almost certainly live out our lives without ever experiencing a sense of having it 'all together.'"

The spirituality of "perfection" that has so long dominated many of our lives—and intimidated them—has given way to a spirituality of desire, of longing, to a spirituality of "incompleteness and contradiction." A spirituality of restlessness.

"It is time," the wise man reminds us, "to look ahead, to forget what is behind, time to pay attention to what you still need, rather than to what you already have."

*"And what is ahead
is a life lived in desire . . ."*

PART THREE
A LIFE LIVED IN DESIRE

At that moment when we realize that what lies ahead of us is a life lived not in fulfillment but in desire, we understand, perhaps for the first time, that our soul's hunger will not—because it cannot—be satisfied this side of complete surrender to God. We realize that it is not just a question of leaving behind an ordinary, decent life. It is about entering into a world and embracing a life unlike anything we have ever known before.

Simply said: if we surrender, we will never again be content to live at a distance from God, even though we may go a lifetime without ever experiencing his presence.

We will enter into a valley of desire, somewhere between the cloud of forgetting and the cloud of unknowing, our heart clinging to where we have been even as it reaches out to what cannot be imagined.

A valley where there is a God, where there is no God.

We will live immersed in mystery.

The pages that follow are meditations on what it is like to live such a life. They are a prayerful introduction to its mysteries, its values, its promises, its pains.

But these words will not take us there. Nor sustain us.

Only love can do that.

A love that is within our reach.

"God forever escapes our power to know. But we have a power to love that is great enough to reach him who is without limits, who forever escapes the power of our mind.

"God can be loved but not imagined. He can be reached and held by our love even as he eludes our thoughts."

Our journey of desire is a journey of love. Not knowledge. Love.

It is so easy, however, too easy, to speak of love. Especially to speak of loving God. But knowing what we are trying to say, what the words mean, is quite another matter.

We want to love God, but don't ask us to understand what this means. In this too we are the unknowing.

But as in everything else about our life with God, we do the best we can. We use the words we have. "Lift up your heart to God," the mystic tells us, "in a simple undiluted act of love . . . with a sharp dart of love and longing." And our heart nods its agreement, borrowing the mystic's words as though we know what we are agreeing to. As though we understand.

But there are some words, some things, we do understand. We know that to love God is above all else to desire God, to long for his presence.

We know this because we know what it is like to hunger for union with another, to close the distance that separates us. To be one. In body and soul.

We know what it is to ache with longing. What it is to stumble over our feelings, to all but drown in our words, to hope beyond hope that we will be understood, that frail and ambiguous as they are, the words we have will be enough, at least for now. That God will understand what we are trying to say. That he will understand our desire, our longing.

We now know that without desire and longing our unknowing will be lifeless, an intellectual exercise, an arid and empty shell, a dark path. Without desire and longing it is a path that leads nowhere.

But where there is desire there is hope. We remember what the nameless monk told the young seeker: "In his great grace he has kindled a desire in your heart to be more closely united to him. He is leading you to himself on a loving leash of longing for a more perfect life."

We need only follow his lead. Need only trust him. But this too is easier said than lived.

Where he takes us may not, will almost certainly not square with our expectations. It may not be where we expected love to lead us, where we wanted love to lead us. Where we would have preferred to go.

He leads us not into security and certainty, but to desire and longing, to a home with the unknowable. He leads us to that place where everything is out on the table, nothing is held back, nothing put on hold, and nothing protected from our fear of the future.

In the valley of desire nothing is put aside in some safe place. There are no exit clauses. No hedging. No conditional clauses, no time clauses, no subclause to limit our gift.

This is what it is like beyond an ordinary, decent life. Here love requires us to let go of everything that until now we have trusted to keep us safe, to make us whole.

Here our longing must turn to trust. A trust without which our desire and our love will evaporate into wishful thinking and sentimental regrets.

The time has come to trust God, to put our lives in the hands of God.

And what does God want of us?

"She wants your undistracted heart.

"He wants you to keep your eyes fixed on him and him alone.

"She wants you to leave her free to act in your soul.

"He wants to be alone with your heart.

"Your job is simply to keep the windows and the doors of your heart closed against everyone and everything that would compete for his love.

"Woo him humbly in prayer.

"He will do everything else.

"He is waiting for you."

From Our Unknown Teacher

Let him do his work in you.
Your only task is to guard
the windows and doors of your soul
against the encroachment of every thing
that could distract you from his love.

Here in the valley of desire
I know that you want from me
nothing more or less than
an undistracted heart.
You want to be
alone with me,
and I with you
my eyes fixed on you
and you alone.
It seems so little to ask,
so little to give.
But you are asking me
to believe that you are enough,
all I will ever need.
It is very hard
for a distracted soul,
for a cautious soul like mine.
Be patient.

I

The Desert

The way of unknowing that has come to us through the centuries is about two clouds— the cloud of forgetting and the cloud of unknowing. But we are more familiar with the vast unnamed spiritual territory that stretches beneath the two clouds. It is a desert where we forget but not perfectly, where we surrender our need to know but not completely, where we live, broken, damaged, wounded, full of contradiction, questions, and hypocrisies, but full too of wonder.

At one moment there is light. At another only darkness. Always a dialogue between the two, always a dialogue of God and our soul.

But whether in darkness or light we live in a desert that stretches beyond our ability to see. There it seems nothing can grow, but there, we discover, nourished by desire and longing, God can take roots

"Sometimes," we have been warned "life in the desert will seem like a foretaste of hell. We will be tempted to despair of ever emerging from the pain of the journey to find a place of rest.

"But there will also be moments when we will feel close to the union we seek because of the joys and consolations that we will experience. We will have a sense of God because of the peace he brings with him."

For the most part, however, we will spend our spiritual life neither in hell nor paradise, but in a desert of desire.

I know something of the desert and what it has to teach. I live where the desert is daily ever more overgrown with development. But I can still find untouched desert just a few miles into the mountains. At a sharp bend in a twisting road there is an overlook where I can pull aside and see still-unspoiled mountains and valleys that stretch all the way to distant and vague horizons.

On any day I can be caught up in the extraordinary silence of the place. In the winter I can look for signs of spring. And in the spring I can see the desert bloom. I can see it come alive with color, with the life that has been for so many months just beneath the arid surface.

Where I stand, the land tumbles sharply away to a valley hundreds of feet below. So I am careful never to come too close to the edge. I remain always a cautious tourist, an onlooker, a sometime visitor. I recognize the desert's beauty and its pull, but always from a distance. I am not a desert dweller. It is too dangerous for me.

For all its beauty, for all its magnetism, I hold back. For all its romance and hints of God, the valley of desire can be a dangerous place. People die here. They drive off its cliffs. They get lost. It is no place for the halfhearted. Or the reckless.

For all its quiet, I sense its danger.

I hold back.

From Our Unknown Teacher

Call upon him,
He will always, at once, come to your aid.
He is most willing
and is only waiting for you.
Why hesitate?

A Prayer of Unknowing

Here in the valley of desire
my heart is a desert,
arid at times,
ablaze with life at others.
Serene at one moment
Dangerously captivated at others.
It is a strange and lonely place,
you present everywhere
but no one in sight.
Hear its silence.
Hear its yearnings.
And its fears.
Understand why it is
that I hold back.
Be patient with my heart.

2

Love and Longing

To speak of a sharp dart of love and longing, of the desire that is at the core of the way of unknowing, may sound at first hearing, or even tenth, like something left over from a lacy valentine. The phrase has about it the smell of rampant sentimentality, a romantic vision of the spiritual journey, a pious excuse to avoid the hard work that we are sure is involved. It sounds like an invitation to reduce spirituality to gloppy sentiment.

It is on the contrary the most radical demand of our spiritual journey.

It is the turning point.

We are being told that the time has come to put our trust in what until now we have considered a mere emotion, and to leave behind our "strengths." It is time to let go of our conviction that we can reach God with the power of our mind and will.

We have come as far as they can take us. At the edge of Unknowing they lose their power. It is time to put them aside. They belong to the Cloud of Forgetting. They are not going to work where we want to go because the darkness will not yield to power.

To pierce the darkness of unknowing only one thing works: the sharp dart of love and longing.

It is not about power but about surrender.

It is not about siege but about laying down our arms.

It is about being defenseless.

It is about living stripped of everything but God.

It is about reducing our life to love and longing.

It is no longer about us, but about God.

Not what we can do, but about what only God can do.

It is a strange feeling, unnerving, even unwelcome. We like to be in charge, in command of our lives, in control.

If the darkness is to be pierced, we would like to take credit for it.

But that's not the way it works. The love and longing of which we speak is not of our doing. It is God at work within us.

Only the sharp dart of love and longing
can cut through the thick darkness
of the cloud of unknowing.

A Prayer of Unknowing

Here in the valley of desire
I want nothing more than
to enter this night
without defenses,
stripped of everything but you,
my life reduced to love and longing.
But I am far from such simplicity.
In my heart of hearts
I still believe that I can reach you
with the power of my mind and will,
that love and longing are not enough.
But they are,
and I know they are
even as I approach you
with my well-defended heart.

3

A Matter of Desire

The idea that the success of our journey of unknowing is not dependent on effort but on desire seems at first ironic if not downright puzzling.

"It is not what you are," we are told, *"nor what you have been that God looks at with his merciful eyes, but what you desire."*

It is a matter of desire—not accomplishment. Desire—not satisfaction. It is a hard standard for us to comprehend, to accept.

It would be difficult enough, God knows, to be measured by the familiar standards of who we are and what we have done, even by what we plan to do. We would understand that. We have, after all, been born into and educated in a culture where we are what we do. Since childhood, we have been encouraged to prove ourselves, to establish our worth, to build a track record, to get an "A." "I have achieved something, therefore I am." Now—in that which matters most—we are told that what we do is not what matters.

But what is even more surprising, perhaps even upsetting, we are told that we will instead be measured by what we "desire." That has always been OK for kids, but a no-no for adults.

Almost inevitably the very word "desire" summons up the kind of childhood daydreaming we have long fought to leave behind. We have been warned again and again that mere desire won't cut it. "Get real. Stop your dreaming."

Now we are told that desire is to be, must become, our way of life.

The word obviously needs to be rescued from its history. And who better to do that than the mystics who have crossed through the valley of desire, who know every step of the way of desire, whose lives defined desire.

For them, as it must become for us, desire was and is *focused passion*. Not the pyschobabble kind of passion that shows up in every celebrity interview, but a life force that centers our existence, that focuses and energizes our journey toward the cloud of unknowing.

A passionate, unremitting desire for what is beyond our understanding, beyond our knowing, becomes the defining center of our lives.

It is a matter of desire—not accomplishment.

Desire—not satisfaction.

From Our Unknown Teacher

It is not what you are
nor what you have been
that God looks at with his merciful eyes,
but what you desire to be.

A Prayer of Unknowing

Here in the valley of desire
release my heart
from the limits
of what my soul can imagine.
It can never be enough.
It need not be.
I do not need to prove myself,
to establish my worth.
I need only to desire
a life beyond my imagining,
beyond the confines of my dreams.
It is not what I am
that I bring to you,
nor what I have been,
but what I desire to be.

4

Forgetting

Catching a glimpse of God, we are tempted to rush headlong toward the heights of mysticism where we are invited to forget everything but God. We kid ourselves that we can bypass all the thousands of small steps along the way.

But we have a long way to go before we get to love's final stages. There is no leapfrogging. Before we breathe the rarefied air of the cloud of unknowing, we have, we are told, a lot of forgetting to do. But, in truth, we find it awkward to make forgetting part of our spiritual vocabulary, even harder to make of it an ideal to be pursued.

After all, in our everyday world, forgetting is closer to carelessness than it is to virtue. It has become almost a synonym for aging. It's a frequent substitute for forgiving.

Given this, one theologian has suggested that forgetting may not quite be the right word for our times and for our stage of spiritual growth.

He has suggested that the right word might be "detachment." He might have suggested "untangling" or "even freeing up."

Whatever word we prefer, however, it is meant to take us far beyond a vocabulary exercise. We are closing in on a central spiritual truth, the need to free ourselves and keep ourselves free from anything and anyone who holds our life captive. Or who might.

There is no question of limiting our forgetting to the bad stuff, the persistent and commonplace entangling stuff of our lives. In the end all of creation is to be forgotten, even the best, even where we glimpse the face of God. But before we get there, we have a lot of forgetting to do.

It's the principle of the thing. It's about keeping the end in view as we take even our most stumbling first steps.

At this stage we are being reminded that anyone and anything can trip us up. We are being warned that something will almost certainly do just this if we do not proceed with a conviction that entering the cloud of unknowing demands of us that we forget everything else but God.

Not because everything else is bad but simply because it isn't God.

We have to confront our own and nature's pretensions to divinity and our natural propensity for idolatry. And unblinkingly face them down.

From Our Unknown Teacher

Think only of him.
Do not let your mind and heart be distracted.
Do everything you can
to set aside
everything that is not God himself.

Here in the valley of desire
I must learn to forget
everything but you.
It will not be easy.
My life, my heart
is cluttered with
the distractions of a thousand days,
and the thousand things
in which I have placed my trust
and my hopes,
and to which
a corner of my heart
still clings.
I need to
untangle my soul.

5

Only God

n a word: I would like God to make his presence felt. I admit it. I am usually uncomfortable—though sometimes relieved—when I don't feel that presence.

And to be honest about it: if God is going to make his presence felt, most of the time I would prefer that it be comforting rather than challenging. Some days my dreams and desires can't take me much farther than my need for a warm blanket.

This is, I know, nothing to be ashamed of. There is more to our God dreaming than dark nights of the soul and the sound of silence. But there is also more to it than how we feel on any given day. After all, God can no more be defined and confined by our uncontrollable and spontaneous feelings than she can be captured by our words.

There are two overlapping questions here, two traps really: confusing God-feelings with God, and confusing God with comfort.

Comfort first: there is nothing wrong about perceiving God as our ultimate source of comfort and wanting God to be just that. The problem comes when we confuse the giver with the gift. It's crucial if we are to take a spiritual path to keep them separate. It's union with God that we want, and it will be only with a great deal of care that we will avoid being content with the beauty of his gifts.

"It is," as our unknown teacher reminds us, "too easy to love God for his gifts. We will know that we have given in to this temptation if we complain when they are taken away."

The other temptation is to confuse our feelings with God's presence, or more exactly with God herself. Not only is God not that warm comfort, she is also none of the feelings that well up within us when we are overcome by the beauty and the strength of her creation. God is not contained in any and all those moments when we so easily detect and celebrate the presence of God, in any or all those moments when the spiritual is at our fingertips. God is not a feeling.

Unless we are very careful, we will conclude on the day that the warmth goes away that God has gone with it.

In the cloud of unknowing there is only God. No stand-ins.

From Our Unknown Teacher

When it comes to
spiritual and emotional consolations,
no matter how closely they seem to bring us to God,
we need to greet them
with a kind of indifference.

A Prayer of Unknowing

Here in the valley of desire
I know it should not matter
whether or not I feel your presence.
But it does.
I want to know
that you are here,
that you are real,
that I am not alone.
I want to feel something,
not just the silence
of the night,
not just the ache of my loneliness,
not just the hunger pains
of my heart.
I know it should not matter.
But it does.
Be near.

6

Prayer

Occasionally in the midst of the quiet dailiness of our desert life there will come moments of startling insight when we will sense with unusual clarity the presence or absence of God, the omnipresence of mystery.

In these moments we may respond spontaneously and in the process learn what it means to pray, what it means to be conscious of mystery. We will be struck all but dumb, left all but speechless. And it will be enough. It is what is meant to be.

But in the same moment there will also be a temptation to reduce our experience to words, to gain control of the moment, and by capturing it in familiar formulas, to shape it to our understanding. We are going to want to say something. It is what we are used to, what we have come to trust.

But it's the wrong time for speeches.

We have caught sight of the flames that are licking at the edge of our life.

It is not a time for meditation. Just a word pulled from our soul will do.

We do what comes naturally. We shout "fire."

We do not pause to strike a pose. We react as our humanity urges us to act. We respond not with memory but with a gasp of delight or fear. We expose our humanity without pretension.

We breathe a single word: God.

We pray.

For more than anything else prayer is our spontaneous response to the mystery of God and of ourselves. To the omnipresence of mystery. To an awareness of the moment that needs no words.

The Spirit is at work within us, to lead us in prayer. And we acknowledge that presence. We follow that lead.

And lest we forget, our unknown teacher is with us, still to remind us that some things don't change.

From Our Unknown Teacher
_____

Most of the time we are reminded of God
and moved to meditation and prayer
by something we read or hear,

or by the sight of something special.
But sometimes a sudden sense of our sinfulness,
or an intuitive insight into God's goodness catches
us by surprise.
We cannot take credit for such moments
as though they were the products
of our own efforts,
a reward for earnest thinking.
They are of God.
So too our meditations and prayers.

We may find ourselves moved to respond
with nothing more
than we can find in a single word like
"God" or "sin."
It will not be a question of having analyzed
insights
or the words that they give rise to.

Nor is it a question of a successful search
for their roots and meanings,
but of letting the grace of God which inspired you
lead you in prayer letting you sink into their
wholeness.

In these moments
a little word of one syllable is better than two,
and more in keeping with the Spirit.

Let your prayers rise directly to God
without meditation.
Do not pause to meditate
or to compose a response.
Do what comes naturally.

Be like those suddenly overcome
by the sight of fire and the danger of death.
They do not take time out to compose paragraphs.
They respond with a single cry.

So should we.

A Prayer of Unknowing

Here in the valley of desire,
if just for a moment,
let me be caught up in the quiet stillness
of your presence.
It is not a time or place
to gather my thoughts,
not a time
to find the right words.
It is a time
to let my heart
rise directly to you.
I need no words,
but here I am,
still reaching for them.
I am a slow learner.

7

Listening

The closer we come to the cloud of unknowing, the less our prayer is a matter of words, the more it is a state of being. A quiet attentiveness. A focus. A simple being in the presence of a God who is.

For many of us, it is not a comfortable place to be. We have been taught to put our trust in the right words. We have come to believe that often as not we must shout in order to be heard, in order to let God know that we exist and what we need.

Now we are being pulled beyond the best of our words to silence, to a wordless encounter with mystery.

Prayer becomes listening, a speechless acknowledgment of God's presence, of our willing surrender to a reality that the daily noise of our life obscures.

We have been told all along that silence is meant to be, from the beginning, a part of our spiritual life. But something happens at this stage of our growth. We are speechless now not as a spiritual exercise but because we recognize that we have come to a place that escapes our every effort at understanding, our very need to understand. We have come not bearing words, but prepared to listen to a God who speaks not in words but by "presence." By sharing his silence.

Our journey to this silence is the beginning of mature prayer, is in itself prayer.

But prayer is not just a place of silence. It is a place where we just "are," a place where we are naked, where no masks are permitted, and no disguises. Where we tell no self-serving lies. Where we are not in control. Where we are always in the moment.

The director Mark Rydel, talking about actors entering into a scene, says that their every instinct is to protect themselves, to keep control of the situation. But this is precisely what they cannot do, what they must not do. The same is true of us when we enter into prayer.

We want to protect ourselves; we want to control the situation. But prayer is about spiritual vulnerability, about defenselessness, about surrender. It is about letting go. It is about spiritual honesty. No one is anxious to be naked to the marrow of his or her soul. Yet this is what prayer demands.

It is where our spiritual journey brings us.

The reward is that we find ourselves in a place where we are totally accepted, where the God into whose presence we have come couldn't care less who we are, insists, in fact, that we come to the moment as we are. She is not interested in seeing someone else. It is who we are that he has been awaiting.

It is a place where our spiritual hunger need not be reduced to the size of our memories and the criteria of others, wherein our nakedness needs no protective covering, where we are loved without limitations, where our soul feels at home. Where our silence has no need to be covered up with words.

Rather than a shelter to which we retreat to get away from the real world, it is the place we go to be most truly and most fully ourselves, to simply be in the presence of a God who simply is.

From Our Unknown Teacher

Prayer is a time
for simply being
in the presence of God who is.

Here in the valley of desire
I admit that
my every instinct is to protect myself,
to raise my defenses,
to stay in control.
But this is what I cannot do,
what I must not do.
Always, too, I look for the right words,
but there are none.
There is only silence
and surrender.
There is only you,
as you are.
Let me be with you,
as I am.

8

Silence and Solitude

For centuries now, ever since the first seekers left the marketplace and retreated to the desert, physical silence and solitude have become the spiritual bread and butter for God-seekers of all the great traditions. They have become fundamental disciplines that are insisted on if we are ever to satisfy our hunger for God, if we are ever to cut through the noise of our lives and into the silence of God, if we are ever to embrace the object of our hope.

We have been told that if we keep quiet long enough and restrict our contact with humanity, we will catch the ear of God.

We have become accustomed to building our spiritual lives around a model of desert and cloistered monastic spirituality with their emphasis on verbal silence and physical solitude. It has been pretty much the only model available, bequeathed in good faith to us by several generations of spiritual teachers and writers because it was pretty much the only model they knew.

But in our own times, silence and solitude have come to seem especially difficult, even unreal. To adopt them as a discipline by those of us who must satisfy our spiritual hunger in a noisy and crowded world—which means most of us—seems at best an invitation to profound frustration.

In such a world—our world—islands of verbal silence and physical solitude smack of wishful thinking, of spiritual unreality. They carry a whiff of elitism—a joke played on our deepest desires. They conjure up fantasies of untroubled, undistracted hooded figures, shaved heads bent in prayer, garden silence everywhere, God palpably present. Nary a child in sight. Nary a time clock measuring our worth.

Our hopes are relegated to a world of spiritual fantasy that has nothing in common with the one in which we live and in which we are required to satisfy our hunger. We could be pardoned for blowing off such a standard.

But unfortunately the monastic model is an ideal that is still alive and well. It is hard to escape the notion that authentic spirituality can only be achieved by turning our homes and workplaces into faux deserts and monasteries with, for good measure, an occasional weekend retreat to the real thing.

The sad thing is that when this doesn't work, and generally it won't, we can too easily abandon any hope of satisfying the God-hunger which rumbles in our soul. Our hope for a life that will free us up and allow us to explore the mystic in all of us can seem to be a futile war with the only world available to us.

We end up settling for much too little because we feel turned away at the door: "only solitaries need apply."

We are tempted to give up a committed spiritual journey that goes beyond a simple decent life because we are not solitaries, not cloistered contemplatives. We are not likely to be. We are just ordinary God-hungry folk busy living up to our life's commitments in a noisy, demanding world where outward silence is not only a luxury far beyond our spiritual means, but a paralyzing roadblock.

Where does this leave us?

It leaves us not with the absence of sound, but with the presence of God.

A presence that cannot be reduced to a voice.

It is not a matter of going somewhere, leaving someplace, straining to hear what cannot be heard. God is where we are—not so much present as he is a presence.

There will be moments of deep silence and there will be places and times of profound solitude. Some sought out, others thrust upon us. But we cannot count on them. They may never be there because in the end they are not necessary. What is necessary for our life in the desert is not voices heard, but a recognition and acknowledgment that we are in the presence—felt or not—of God.

What we can do is, if just for a moment now and then, still the noises within.

We can unclutter our hearts.

We can get out of God's way.

We can offer the silence of our own heart.

We can—we must—as our unknown teacher tells us, forget, leave behind all our expectations, all our preconceptions of who we are, of who God is, of what awaits us in whatever silence and solitude we can find.

From Our Unknown Teacher

[Do not] squander your moments of
silence and solitude
By bringing to your prayers
your stored up notions
of what you are or what God is.

Here in the valley of desire
our moments of silence and solitude
are precious and rare.
My life and my world rush in to fill them
with their presence, their demands,
reducing silence
to words I can understand
and solitude to loneliness.
But I go on looking for a silence
the world cannot give,
for a solitude
that cannot be found where I expect it
but only within
a silenced heart
that is comfortable
alone with you.

9

Consent

Our relationship with God—regardless of whether it is lived in a valley of desire or in a cloud of unknowing—is always a gift that we consent to. Nothing more, nothing less, and never anything else.

God gives us something. Freely.

That's the fact.

But it is a gift that is never fully revealed, never fully unwrapped, never understood. It is the gift of unknowing.

We can say that God is giving us herself. But that doesn't help. It just covers up the mystery with words, just buries it deeper.

God is present. That is the gift. We consent to that presence. Or we don't. In either case: "God as he must is doing his work within us."

We consent or we don't.

We acquiesce or we don't.

We surrender or we don't.

We let go or we don't.

But the work goes on.

With or without us.

We need to know, to accept, that our consent is not a matter of entering into a contract in which each side gets to establish its limits, its contents, and its clauses. Its terms are not reached after a bargaining session. There is no sunset clause. The process is not one of establishing terms, of coming to an agreement with God. "We have a deal!" It is a matter of unconditional consent, unconditional acquiescence, unconditional surrender, without any knowledge of what is being agreed to, what is being surrendered or to whom.

We are not partners. We are not in the know. We are the unknowing.

God isn't looking for our help, just our consent, our willingness to get out of the way. God is looking for our willingness to clear the cluttered landscape of our soul, to untangle ourselves from the twisted branches that threaten to trip us at every step, the branches that have grown wild over years of tolerance, of neglect, of familiarity—that have accumulated into the brambles of our lives.

Our role is simply to get out of God's way, to make room for God to do what only God can do.

It's not that easy. More to the point, it is not all that flattering to our spiritual ego.

It is the opposite of "doing for our self."

It is the opposite of holding on, the opposite of controlling our spiritual destiny.

We are consenting to let God do what only God can do. And when we try to switch roles, to do the impossible and discover that it can't be done, we have no choice but to settle for what little we can accomplish on our own. Which isn't much. We end up getting stuck in our childhood. We stop growing.

We would rather be the carpenter than the wood. But that's not the way it is with God's gift. It's not what we are consenting to.

We are consenting to being led, but we don't know where.

From Our Unknown Teacher

God as he must is doing his work within you.
Let him lead you, as he will.
He needs only your consent.
And that you stay out of his way.
Do not try to help him along

Lest you spoil what he is attempting to do
in and for you.
You be the wood. He the carpenter.

A Prayer of Unknowing

Here in the valley of desire
remind me
that it is not me but you
who is at work within me,
that it depends
not on me,
but you.
Lead me as you will.
You need only my consent.
And that I stay out of your way.
Don't let me get in the way of
what you are attempting to do
in and for me.
I am not the carpenter.
I am the wood.
Shape me.

10

Doing

In the early days of our spiritual journey there is an understandable desire, even impatience, to know what we should do next. With an emphasis on the "do." In the latter days of our journey, more likely than not, our humanity will still insist on emphasizing the "do." Our confidence in "doing" doesn't melt away.

After all, doing has been the signature of our humanity. "I do, therefore I am." So what shall I *do* now?

Follow your heart. Go where it takes you. Prayer and good works are the spontaneous and necessary outpouring of a heart that is in the right place. They are the practice darts of love directed at the darkness in front of us and around us. They are God prompting us. They foreshadow a life lived in the cloud of unknowing.

Do all these things and more because not even the most fervent contemplative is excused from the love and service of his neighbor. Nor from the ongoing need to remind himself of God's presence.

But it doesn't matter, our teacher reminds us, "how much you fast, what vigils you keep, how early you rise, how hard your bed, or rough your hair shirt . . . nor how many tears you shed for your sins.

"Without the simple love and longing for God that comes to rest in the dark cloud of unknowing, they matter very little."

What matters is that spontaneous dart of love and longing which alone carries us into the cloud of unknowing. It is not the product of *our* doing but rather the work of God within us. It alone can pierce the darkness.

But here's the rub. We can't—most of us—escape a feeling that because we are not doing something, nothing is happening. We feel a need to measure our lives. Without any benchmarks to measure our progress, we are at a loss.

But something is happening, even when we are doing nothing.

It's just happening in the dark.

We are being given our first taste of life in the cloud of unknowing.

Little by little we will come to depend less and less on what we do, on what we can do. We will get used to living in the dark. Living free of the yardstick of our accomplishments.

From Our Unknown Teacher

There are many things
that we might consider of great good to us,
but by comparison with a blind impulse of love
there is little they can or may do.

A Prayer of Unknowing

Here in the valley of desire
I am still keeping score.
It is a hard habit to break.
If I do this
and multiply that
I will earn your love.
Remind me again
that it is not what I do that matters
but what you do in me.
I have a bad memory.
You will need to remind me again tomorrow.

II

God Simply Is

Our unknown teacher tells us that we must rid our soul of everything that is not God, even of the gifts of God that enchant our heart, even the beauties of his creation that have led us to where we are, to where we want to be.

Put them aside, we are told. Think solely of God in himself. Not *what* God is, just *that* God is.

But how do we go about thinking solely of God in himself?

We don't.

We can't.

When pressed, our unknown teacher admits: "I have no idea."

We have come to the cloud of unknowing, where ideas don't count. And we wonder: what are we doing here where even saints would fear to tread?

We are here because our ideas, our words have brought us as far as they can, which isn't far enough. What we know, what we can know is not enough to satisfy our deepest hungers.

What is important is that we have been brought to the very edge of what we can achieve, of what we can take credit for, the outer edges of our knowledge and our skills. It is not just that we are silent and speechless, even wordless in the presence of God—it is that we are without answers.

In things that have always mattered to us, upon which we have always depended, we are powerless.

Beyond this point the best we can say is this: "I have no idea." It is a humbling moment. It is meant to be.

"In itself," our unknown teacher tells us, "humility is nothing else but our true understanding and awareness of ourselves as we truly are."

It is in this moment that we are meant to see, accept, and love ourselves as we are, speechless, powerless.

But there is one other thing . . . we are beloved by God.

Our humility is born not just in our powerlessness, but in the "superabundant love and worthiness of God himself."

Nothing is more humbling than recognizing and accepting the fact that we are loved without question, loved as we are, loved without cause, loved without merit.

In the face of such a gift "all nature trembles, all learned men are fools, and all the saints and angels are blinded." A humility takes root in our soul that is at once a recognition of our powerlessness and the empowering love of God, a humility whose reality is at once as fragile and passing as our own understanding of our worth, and as perfect and lasting as the love of God.

"How do I go about entering the cloud of unknowing?"

I must answer: "Humbly."

From Our Unknown Teacher

You have a right to ask me:
"How do I go about thinking of God in himself?"
I must answer:
"I have no idea."

Here in the valley of desire
I am told that I am loved by you,
that I am loved
with the "superabundant love and worthiness
of God himself."
But how can this be?
I am told that
I must think about you,
just as you are in yourself,
setting aside even the gifts
in which I catch a glimpse of your beauty
and your love,
of your very being.
But how can this be?
I must answer:
"I do not know.
I cannot know."

12

The Sacred

We humans have a bad habit of tagging certain parts of creation as sacred. And others as not. Some places, some people are set-aside, con-secrated, made sacred. A burial ground. A battlefield. A piece of cloth called a flag. A monarch. A priest. A relationship. A marriage. Sex. They are to be approached shoeless, knee-bent, with lowered eyes. They are set aside by human decree as places and situations where you can expect to find God.

On a good day the rest is labeled profane—secular, worldly, disrespectful of what is holy—a case of "close, but no cigar," good enough but not a meeting with God. On a bad day it is labeled sinful and declared totally off limits to God and anyone looking for him.

God, however, if I read the various scriptures correctly, didn't divide creation into good and evil, sacred and profane. He did what he did, made what he made, and "saw that it was good." All of it. All the time. To everyone.

It is all sacred—even the small stuff. Not because someone, or some institution declares it so, but because God made it so.

God never says: "I'll be here, not there." She never says: "Not now, come back later." She never asks: "Do I know you?" God is not "for display purposes only—don't touch."

God is available to all of us. Everywhere we are. As who we are.

Repeat after God: "I saw that it was good." There are no little things. There is no "small stuff." In the end none of it is profane. It is all sacred.

But there is something more. The unknown monk reminds us that it's all sacred, but it just isn't God.

And sacred though it may be, it isn't enough. Our restless hearts may be tempted, will be tempted daily to stop somewhere in the valley of desire and call it enough.

But it isn't enough, because it isn't God.

Nothing in God's creation can satisfy the hunger of our heart, or the desire that centers our soul. Because nothing short of God can.

This is the heart of unknowing.

We have to detach ourselves from a sacred, God-permeated world if we are to attach ourselves without strings to its creator, if we are to go from the knowable to the Unknowable.

We have to let go.

So "while it is a good thing sometimes to think of the goodness of God, it is more important to lose these thoughts in a cloud of detachment."

But there is something else to remember. We are called upon to detach ourselves from creation without demonizing it. We are asked to detach ourselves from even the good things of creation not by denying they are good, not because they are evil, but simply because they are not enough.

To repeat the words of our nameless teacher:

"Our task now is the hard and unending one of putting behind us, of consigning to a cloud of forgetting, all that must be put aside if we are to approach unknowing, if we are to love God and God alone."

From Our Unknown Teacher

While it is a good thing sometimes
to think of the goodness of God,
it is more important to lose these thoughts
In a cloud of detachment.

A Prayer of Unknowing

Here in the valley of desire
I need to remember that
nothing in your creation
can satisfy the hunger of my heart,
or the desire that centers my soul.
Because nothing short of you can.
You permeate your world.
You are everywhere I see or touch or feel.
But it is not you.
So it is not enough.
I am tempted to stop here
in the valley of desire,
and believe that your world is enough.
But only you are enough,
my heart must not stop short of you.

13

The Stumbling Block

wonder if there is any passage in the whole of spiritual literature more likely to confuse us— even upset us—than the one where our need to understand is called "a stumbling block."

It is comparatively easy for us to accept that the life attracting us is one that is not just beyond our understanding but beyond what is understandable.

It is just as easy in the quiet warmth and confidence of our prayer and our first enthusiasm to want nothing more than to reach out to God in simple love and to choose a life lived in such a union.

What is far less easy for us is that in respond-ing to God's invitation, in choosing such a life, our basic urge to understand, a cornerstone of our humanity, will no longer be a source of pride and energy but a "powerful stumbling block to our attempts to reach God in simple love."

We are being asked for the sake of union with God to leave behind—to forget—what we have spent a lifetime cultivating. We are being asked to overcome our need to make sense, to set aside our perpetual pursuit of meaning, to overcome the driving character of our humanity, our intense need to understand.

We are being asked to resist our very human efforts to capture God.

We are being cautioned to distrust any moment—in fact, to turn around and flee—when we have the feeling that we understand it all.

Spirituality is never about understanding. It is always about "not understanding."

It is about surrendering to mystery, to the unknown and the unknowable.

It is at this point that we begin to understand how profound, even radical, is our decision to accept God's invitation to take up our spiritual residence in a cloud not of knowing but of unknowing.

"Help me understand" becomes "help me to live without understanding."

This can be slippery country.

Venturing into a life of unknowing will seem to some the equivalent of abandoning reason, proof of what many have long suspected and frequently charged, that to choose a spiritual path is to lose our mind, to abandon our intelligence at the doorstep of a mature life.

But others who have chosen to enter the cloud of unknowing see it differently. Not to choose a life of unknowing is to pull back from the full potential of our humanity. It is to settle for what our very limited minds can achieve and encompass. It is settling for what we should be forgetting.

It is settling for far too little.

This is not just a slippery time, it is a scary moment.

Do we really want to go where our mind cannot take us, where we must let go of the security that our hard-earned understanding has brought us? Our dreams may be too little, but perhaps, we think, they may be enough. Do we really want to take the next step?

We hear our souls answering yes.

Whatever the cost.

From Our Unknown Teacher
_____

Our intense need to understand
will always be a powerful stumbling block
to our attempts to reach God in simple love
and must always be overcome.

A Prayer of Unknowing

Here in the valley of desire
let me not stumble over
my need to understand.
Rather
than settling for what
my mind can achieve and encompass,
let me choose instead
a life of unknowing.
Let me choose you,
who are unknowable
rather than a God of my creation,
a God shrunk to my size.
Let me choose instead
to be fully human,
to be unknowing

14

Our Only Power

With the power of the mind we can set out to tame the world around us, describe its depths, name its inhabitants, unlocking as we go piece after piece of the universe. We can unravel what has been secret since the beginning of time. We can make sense. Our world is relatively within our control.

But in reaching out to her who is without limits, we must accept that, in this pursuit, to depend on the power of our mind is to be powerless.

Ultimately the only power we have in the valley of desire is the power of love. Only love, we are told, is enough to pierce the darkness. But to depend on our definition of love, and our experiences of it, is to be left every bit as powerless. It is to be left at the mercy of a word that has been made almost meaningless by overuse and misuse, and so distorted by the human baggage it carries that it needs to be left behind, consigned to the cloud of forgetting.

So when we hear all this talk of love, it is right to feel uneasy. We should proceed with caution—and humility. A love that is defined by and within the limits of our humanity is not a love capable of piercing the darkness, of reaching her who is without limits.

Only God's love can do that.

So when, in fact, we reach out to him who is without limits, it is God who must do the reaching for us. The blind, indefinable stirring that lights up the darkness, that darts to the very center of our being to reveal God's presence within the darkness, the stirring that we call love is in fact not of our making. It is God at work within us.

In love too we are the unknowing.

But even so there is something we do know.

The power that we need to reach him who is without limits is already present and at work within us. And real.

It needs only our consent.

From Our Unknown Teacher
_____

The power of love in each of us
is great enough to reach
him who is without limits,
who forever escapes the power of our mind.

A Prayer of Unknowing

Here in the valley of desire
I desire only this:
to find within myself
a love strong enough
to pierce the darkness,
strong enough to break through
the cloud of unknowing,
strong enough to go
where only love can go.
Here in the valley of desire
I have no power
but the power of love,
but that is enough,
to reach you.

15

Leaving Self Behind

"When everything else has been consigned to a cloud of forgetting," our unknown teacher tells us, "we are left with a simple awareness and experience of our own self."

It is not a comfortable place to be. It can, in fact, be, as our wise teacher warns us, a place of "almost unbearable sorrow." Our valley of desire can easily, sadly become a land of disappointment.

It happens in that moment when we realize that we have come all this way, have come so close to the fulfillment of our deepest desire only to find in our self-awareness that we are the ultimate obstacle to the union that has been the central quest of our lives.

We have sought in the cloud of forgetting to rid ourselves of everything, to forget everything that is not God, only to come face to face with the greatest obstacle of all, our self.

It is not something possessed or achieved and now forgotten but the self that stands in our way, that blocks our union with God, that frustrates our deepest desires and turns them into sorrows.

And this will remain so for as long as self, not God, continues to be the center of our life.

It will be comparatively easy for us to understand the truth of this moment, but let us make no mistake: such a recentering of our lives will "require of us a very special and rare gift of God's grace and a capacity on our part that is just as rare."

The self-centeredness that we acknowledge goes far deeper than common selfishness. We are not talking about improving our manners.

We are talking about refocusing our lives, about removing self from the equation that defines the meaning of our life.

We are talking about getting out of the way. Getting out of God's way. Getting out of our own way.

We are talking about relocating the center of our existence, which until now has been our self. It will not be easy. Surrender never is.

It is not just a matter of our personal history. It is a matter of the world in which we live, out of which we must make some sense. Ours is a world fixated on self—self-help, self-fulfillment, self-realization, self-consciousness, self-awareness, self-esteem. Anything but self-surrender. In this world our most meaningful journey, we are told, is the one that we travel in search of a lost, damaged, inadequate sense of self. Self is the troubled treasure to be recovered, healed, and celebrated—anything but surrendered.

In the cloud of forgetting we sought to rid ourselves of everything that was not the self we wished to be. As we approach the cloud of unknowing, we are faced with a self that is free of what must be forgotten only to discover that we have finally reached that which stands most powerfully in the way of our desire: the self at the center of our desire.

But here and now in the valley of our desire we have—in Pogo's memorable insight—met the enemy and it is us. It is self.

Only in this recognition do we begin to understand how deep is the change demanded of us. Our self-fixation, our self-centeredness must now give way to God-centeredness.

It does not help that in our world, which as often as not borrows its categories and vocabulary from psychology, self is not, as it is for our unknown teacher, the ultimate spiritual problem. It is not the ultimate obstacle to a spiritual life, but the core of a spirituality that begins and ends with an effort to shore up our ego.

We begin to understand how treacherous our journey will be through the valley that separates the cloud of unknowing from the cloud of forgetting.

We stand in our own way. We block our own passage because we are still at the center of our existence. We keep getting in our own way.

Ironically, in many bookstores spirituality finds itself relegated to the section marked "self-help." The irony is not just that spirituality takes us where we can't help ourselves, where we are in fact most profoundly helpless, but that in the valley of desire we come to know and accept that this emphasis on self scuttles our very journey.

However frightened we might be, we come to accept that the self is not our helper or something to be helped or strengthened. Rather it is something to be left behind.

From Our Unknown Teacher

We are the ultimate obstacle
to the union
that has been the central quest
of our lives.

A Prayer of Unknowing

Here in the valley of desire
I reach out to you
only to find the way blocked
by my self.
I stand in my own way.
I block my own passage.
I frustrate my own deepest desires
and turn them into sorrows.
I need to get out of the way,
your way,
my way.
I need to stand aside.
I am the obstacle.
I admit it.
Remove it—
if I will let you.

16

Why So Little?

I t is easy for us to forget that "in our spirit we are not limited to what we can understand or imagine."

We restrict our dreams, limiting them to the familiar, to what we can see, to what we can measure. We seem unable or unwilling to respond to an invitation to live our life beyond our limited horizons. Instead we rein in our desires, forgetting that while we are limited in our humanity we have no such limitations in the life of our spirit. We overlook that there is nowhere our spirit cannot go—no desire that is beyond our capacity to dream.

This life of the spirit invites us, awaits us.

Yet we hesitate to go there. We cling to our limitations. We stifle our spiritual imagination and any sense of spiritual adventure. We avoid, it seems, getting beyond, living beyond what we can see and hear, beyond the familiar world where we are comfortable.

We play it safe. We hang back. But why?

Why do we who claim to hunger for God hold back from his promise of fuller life? Why do we settle for so little, the little we have and know?

Our heart knows the answer. We feel safer with the God we think we know than with the Unknown God, the Unknowable God who calls to us. We feel safer fenced in by our human limitations than with the prospects of life beyond our understanding and imagination.

So we let our fear of the unknown and the unknowable capture our soul. We give in to our fear of the dark and the risk that it entails. We stand on the edge of unknowing and retreat as often as not to what we know, to what we are comfortable with.

We choose a spirituality that pretty much leaves us where it finds us, tied firmly to our human limitations.

We limit our spirit to what we can know and imagine. And we are the losers for it.

A fullness of life awaits us in the thick darkness of the cloud of unknowing.

From Our Unknown Teacher

When it comes to putting words
to the life of the spirit,
we are limited by our humanity
to what we can understand or imagine.
But in our spirit we are not limited
to what we can understand or imagine.

A Prayer of Unknowing

Here in the valley of desire
I feel safer
with the God I think I know
than with the unknown God,
the unknowable God
who calls to me
to abandon my safety.
I feel safer
fenced in by my human limitations,
than exposed to your promises
of life in a cloud of unknowing.
Remind me
that my spirit is not limited,
only my imagination.

17

The Dark

I t is easy to accept that our spiritual journey will begin in darkness. Even that it will proceed in darkness.

What is difficult for us—almost impossible—is to choose darkness, to accept that darkness is the heart of the matter, that our journey will end in darkness, that our goal is not to break through the darkness to light, but to go deeper and deeper into the darkness.

We are being asked to let go of a world where we think we know how to live, and live in a world where we celebrate our unknowing. We are being asked to leave behind the experience of God's presence to enter into and to live in what John of the Cross called "the dark night of the soul."

It is much easier said than done, so much easier in fact that there is an ongoing danger of reducing this darkness to a concept, our unknowing to a theological formula or a romantic metaphor. There is a danger that we will choose the metaphor over the reality, that our words will become an escape hatch from the darkness of unknowing.

There is a danger that the whole matter of unknowing will become an interesting, tantalizing concept to be played with, an idea that can be substituted for the real darkness. A source of intellectual "good feelings."

But when we say "unknowing" we mean quite literally "not knowing." We mean simply and concretely that we don't know where we are going, where our surrender will take us. It is to go through our days and nights without any real sense of God's reassurance.

But there is nothing romantic about a life spent in the dark, nothing feel-good about everyday life lived in real darkness, about days lived without really knowing what the darkness covers.

It's no fun, no place for warm fuzziness.

Thérèse of Lisieux said of this darkness: "It is not a veil. It is a wall which reaches to the very heavens, shutting out the starry skies."

It is not only unromantic, it is undramatic.

It's the way so many of us live without having a name for it. We do not see the face of God or walk in his blazing presence. His voice is at best muffled. Others talk about their faith, their religious experience, their sense of God—but when we are honest about it, we wonder what they are talking about.

We walk in the dark, hoping for the light. We keep hoping to find a God we can understand. And we presume for the most part that this is just the way things are, just the way it is supposed to be.

We are not quite ready to shake off our fear of the dark.

We are not quite ready for a God we cannot understand.

Ready or not, this is precisely what we have to do.

We have to choose darkness and the mystery that it reveals. We have to accept them as the heart of the matter, as our spiritual destiny, recognizing that our task is not to break through the darkness to light and understanding, but to embrace the dark and what we cannot know.

From Our Unknown Teacher

We have to accept that if we are to experience God in this life it will always be in darkness, in a cloud of unknowing.

Here in the valley of desire
help me to embrace
the darkness that surrounds me,
that pulls me,
that promises me so much.
Help me to overcome my fear of the dark
and the unknown.
For you are
where they are
and if I am to find you
in this life
it will only be in darkness,
in a cloud of unknowing.

18

Stripped of Ideas

The terms of our admission into the cloud of unknowing are as clear as they are demanding.

"Bring nothing with you."

"Get rid of your gods."

"Smash your idols."

"Strip yourself of all the ideas of God that stand like idols between you and the God who invites you, who awaits you—all the ideas of God that have been the subject of your prayers, the object of your hope, the strength that you have borrowed—but which have been only ideas of the unknowable."

"All the gods you have known must die so that the unknowable God can live."

There is no cloaking the message. However you phrase it, it is unmistakable. We are being invited to surrender unconditionally. We come naked or not at all.

Stripped naked, we begin to grasp how deep and radical is the transformation that is being offered to us.

We are like a soldier or a cleric stripped of rank and honors, of reputation, of public identity and dignity. We are stripped of how we see ourselves.

We are like a piece of furniture in the hands of a skilled carpenter, stripped of accumulated layers of paint and varnish until the underlying wood, with all its fault lines and its natural beauty, is revealed.

We are lovers stripped of our clothing and our masks to reveal the naked availability of our mutual surrender

We are without makeup.

We are defenseless, vulnerable.

The images are powerful and provocative, and there is truth in each of them. Sometimes it is a moment of humiliation. At all times it is a moment of surrender and honesty.

In every case, something we have learned to value, something we have come to depend upon, is stripped away to reveal something that is more basic, less adorned, less protected, less secure.

Naked, stripped of our ideas and images, we are totally exposed, utterly vulnerable with a feeling, a fear that in abandoning our ideas of God we are defenseless. We have nothing to rely on. "You mean that wasn't God?"

But naked, "Godless," stripped of preconceptions, we can experience God as he really is.

And for the first time experience ourselves as we can be. As we are meant to be.

It is a scary and rewarding time.

But there are no substitutes.

From Our Unknown Teacher

Only when you are stripped of your ideas
can God let you know and experience him
as he really is.
Only then can he let you know and experience
yourself as you really are.

A Prayer of Unknowing

Here in the valley of desire
it is easy to ask you
to strip me of my ideas of you,
but the reality of what I ask

is almost unbearably frightening.
I want to know you
as you really are.
I want to know myself as I really am.
But I have grown accustomed
to a world of undemanding gods,
of ideas and images I have created
in the image and likeness of myself.
They must die so that you can live in me
and I in you.
As you are.
As I am.

19

Humility

In popular parlance—and practice—humility gets confused with modesty—with knowing our place, with not getting above ourselves. It gets reduced to good manners and never gets much beyond the "Ah shucks, me?" stage.

But humility is not merely a polite response, a social nicety. It is a way of living with the truth, living truthfully with the person we see in the mirror, the person we acknowledge for better or worse when no one else is around to shape or change our mind

More to the point, humility is not about thinking less of our self but rather of gaining a true understanding and awareness of who and what we really are.

It is about telling the truth—and living the truth—for better or for worse, as far as we know it.

And there's the rub. "As far as we know . . ." is not far enough.

We are left on the surface of our lives because our self-understanding can only go as far and as deep as the power of our knowing can take us. And as long as we are confined to the land of knowing, to what we know, to what we can know, our image of ourselves can never be more than a pale shadow of the truth. And our humility can never be more than a reflection of our limitations.

True humility begins only when, with a burst of love, we pierce the cloud of unknowing and discover for the first time the truth about ourselves. We are loved with an extravagant love. A love without limits. A love that has not, cannot be earned. In that moment perfect humility is born in our lives.

From Our Unknown Teacher

. . . a love before which all creation trembles,
all learned men are fools,
all the angels and saints are blinded.

Here in the valley of desire
that person I see in the mirror
is for better or worse
someone who is loved
with an extravagant love.
How can that be?
When I look
all I see
is someone who is hard-pressed
to find anything
that God could love.
But tell me again
that it is true.
And show me how to walk humbly
in that truth.

20

The Desire to Love

It is not just that we desire, with a sharp dart of love, to pierce the darkness that surrounds God, it is that we live with the profoundly human need to name our love and proclaim it, to find the right words, any words for it.

But it's not going to happen.

Here in the valley of desire there comes a moment when, as the mystic says, there arises in the soul a movement that it is at a loss to describe. We become all but speechless. Mystery all but swamps us. Our need to find words plunges us into the very core of unknowing. There is nothing, we realize, that we can say, no words we can use that can measure up to the truth of our lives, the mystery that envelopes us, the God who awaits us, who lives within us but always out of reach of our words.

There are no words to accompany love's arrow.

It is here in this moment of love and speechless desire that we begin to comprehend: the truth is unfathomable, its name unspeakable; our way must be the way of unknowing.

It is here that we begin to comprehend that our destiny is to love but not to know.

It is the most human of moments—the most fragile and the most perplexing.

Unknowable mystery is our lot, the lot of every lover. Our desire to love stumbles over our desire for loving words, for something we can say, for something that will bridge the separation we feel. We learn to accept, however, that our task is not, after all, to find the right words but to come to terms with the silence of love, the presence of God.

The more we love, the deeper a mystery our love becomes. And as our love grows, our unknowing grows. We seem to know less even as we know more. Words become ever less important. Silence deepens. That which "goes without saying" becomes love's sharpest arrow.

"We have to be content not to see," our teacher tells us, "and be willing to put aside our need to know that God is at work within us."

There comes a moment
when there arises in the soul
a movement that we are
at a loss to describe.
It moves us to desire
we know not what,
only that it is
beyond our imagining.

*Here in the valley of desire
let me be content to be speechless,
free,
at least for a moment,
of all the words and images
that clutter my soul,
that blind me to your presence,
that stand in your way.
Help me to feel at home
with what I do not know,
with what I cannot know.
For it is only in the dark,
only in silence
only in my surrender,
that you are visible.*

21

Others

In the course of our journey through the valley of desire we are pursued by a powerful urge to find and settle into a comfortable corner, one just big enough for God and "me." As often as not, we are overtaken by this urge. We are tempted to think that achieving such isolated comfort, if not the whole point of our spiritual journey, is at least as far as our spiritual ambition will carry us.

We want not just to be with God but to be *alone* with God—securely behind a doorway clearly marked "Private."

But here's the rub—we can never be alone with God.

God arrives in our souls accompanied by the whole human race. Past, present, and future. We are meant to keep the same company.

Still it remains an inviting trap and a natural mistake for those of us who are encountering—whether for the first time or even the tenth—the demands, the riches, and the strong attraction of a life of unknowing.

It's a trap because at first glance a safe and secure life is precisely what "spirituality" seems to promise, and what our hearts seek. The very word has a history that smacks of disengagement, of flight from everyday reality. That comfortable corner is a hiding place. An escape hatch. It's just what we ordered.

It is a costly mistake, however, because it so completely misses the point. The spiritual journey is not a way out of our humanity. It is not disengagement, not a matter of shrinking our world. It is not disembodiment, but a constant deepening of our hunger, an aching search for a life that is more fully, more abundantly human.

It is not meant to seal us off from our everyday world, but to open us up, not to constrict our heart, but to expand it. It is not about finding that comfortable corner, however attractive it might be.

One more thing it isn't. It isn't an "inner" life. Our spiritual journey is not a journey "inward."

These attempts at finding words for the mystery of our search are singularly unhappy, because they are so easily and so frequently taken literally. The result is that our reaching inward to God can rapidly turn into a stultifying self-centeredness that is easily mistaken for spiritual growth.

We suffocate. Our "inner" world is not big enough to house our God, to feed our hunger. Our "inner" life ends up betraying our humanity, turning our comfortable corner into a spiritual prison. Not only are we cut down to size, but so is God.

The "inner" journey is a journey into what is, after all, a very small world that leaves, if we are not careful, very little room for anyone or anything else. In the end it is too small even to harbor the presence of God let alone all those that he brings with him. We are left very lonely indeed.

If we are to grow we have no alternative to abandoning any notion of spending our days alone with God. Forget comfortable corners along the way.

Our destiny, our only hope, is to throw our lives wide open and acknowledge that when God comes along, she isn't alone.

From Our Unknown Teacher

All of humanity
is part of our family.
All are our friends
No one is a stranger.

Here in the valley of desire,
even as I pray,
I am looking for some place to
rest my soul,
some place to be alone
with you.
But that's not where you are.
I will find you
with your family
that is now my family
with your friends
who are now my friends,
where there can be no strangers.
Only in their company,
in your company,
can I find rest.

22

Humanity

Like it or not, our humanity follows us wherever we go, even into the cloud of unknowing.Some understand that there is no other way. But many of us don't. Some, in fact, seem to think that leaving our humanity behind is the whole point of a spiritual life.

We are, after all, not talking about an abstract, philosophically sanitized prayer-time humanity, but the faltering, gritty, finite, fickle-hearted humanity that is, if not our pride, certainly our nature, our history, and our very being. It is a gathering of lots of things that we would like to escape from, that we would just as soon consign to the cloud of forgetting.

Sexuality is very high on that list if not at the very top.

We find it hard to put sexuality and spirituality in the same sentence unless on the one hand it is to frame them as irreconcilable enemies, or on the other to sanitize and romanticize the earthiness of both.

It is important to talk about this because the history of spirituality is weighed down with fear of the body—read: fear of sex—that has frequently passed over into contempt and hatred. Those who have been our teachers have almost without exception stayed clear of the human body and its language. They have made celibacy a cornerstone not just of their own spiritual journey, but of all spirituality.

They will reassure us that there is, of course, nothing wrong with sex. But we shouldn't count on having a sex life *and* admission to the cloud of unknowing.

There are some things, however, no matter how much we would prefer to leave them behind, that we cannot consign to the cloud of forgetting without endangering our entrance into the cloud of unknowing.

Our finitude, our humanity, is inseparable from our identity.

We face God with the same humanity with which we face the day—not suddenly knowing, not miraculously secure, not certain, not disembodied. But limited to the very core of our being.

And though it is understandable that we might want to shuck that humanity, God does not respond by rescuing us from our selves, by freeing us of the frail humanity that we bring to him.

We are human. We will always be human. In or out of the cloud of unknowing. If this makes us uncomfortable—so be it. It is not something we have a choice about. It is who we are.

Our humanity, our fragility, our imperfection, our spiritual cowardice is a fact—a burdensome fact that is easily overlooked or deliberately ignored in our desire to live a spiritual life.

We are careful not to put it this way—but we harbor a suspicion, a hope, that in pursuing a spiritual life, a life in the cloud of unknowing, the burden of our humanity will be lifted, that we will become what we are not, that we will be rescued from our human frailty.

We harbor an unspoken hope that spirituality will turn out to be our escape hatch. And as long as we harbor that hope, as long as we put our trust in a bodiless spirituality, our spirituality will be on hold.

But even as refusing to accept our humanity becomes an invitation to spiritual paralysis, choosing to live with and celebrating the fact that we are human, that we are by definition limited, becomes a cornerstone of our life in the valley of desire and in the cloud of unknowing.

We have taken a solid first step into the cloud of unknowing. We have brought our limited, unknowing humanity with us. Knowing only that we shall not know, that God will not replace our unknowing with knowing, our humanity with divinity.

We have come to that place where only humans need apply. Where our humanity is not reduced, but fulfilled.

From Our Unknown Teacher
_____

God forbid
that we should separate
what God has joined together
our bodies and our souls.
It is God's will
that we serve him
with the fullness of our humanity,
and that we should be blessed with joy
in both body and soul.

Here in the valley of desire,
if I am to leave something behind,
if I am to forget something,
let it not be my humanity,
my finitude,
my body.
Let me come to you whole,
body and soul
joined together,
as you meant them to be.
Let me serve you
with the fullness of my humanity,
unfrightened, unembarrassed
blessed with joy,
in both body and soul.

23

Walls

Very few things in and about the spiritual life create greater stumbling blocks than our own expectations.

We expect to discover a certain kind of God. In the wake of that discovery we expect to experience a certain kind of life. The result is that we stumble over our own fantasies.

We can be so busy spinning images of God that God doesn't have a chance to be God.

We can be so busy living out our idea of a spiritual life that we miss the one God has in store. Maybe God has different spiritual lives in store for people of differing circumstances? At different moments in history. At different moments in our lives. One may be as fulfilling as another. We don't know. Because we cannot know what God has in store for any of us.

One thing is certain: nowhere does God say that we are destined for a joy ride.

Thérèse of Lisieux wrote that if we were to judge her solely by her poems, we might think she was a child for whom the veil of faith was all but dissolved. That there was nothing between her and the face of God. That her spiritual life, that all spiritual living, was—is—all sweetness and light. And *that*, we come to expect, is the way it should be. If it doesn't happen that way we must be doing something wrong.

"But it is not a veil," she wrote. "It is a wall that reaches to the very heavens, shutting out the starry skies."

She lived with walls, not transparent veils. She lived with raw, unsweetened faith. "I feel no joy," she wrote. " I sing only of what I wish to believe."

And if we can bear to admit it, this is the way it is for most if not all of us, for most if not all our days. We live with walls, not with transparent veils. We find little or no joy.

Spirituality is about faith. It is about walls. It is about living without seeing, living without knowing. It is about accepting that no matter how right we get it, the walls will not come tumbling down.

They are not supposed to.

Centuries before Thérèse, in a similar desire to find words for this mystery, a nameless teacher talked not about walls, but about a cloud of unknowing.

Neither wall nor cloud will go away.

Neither can be stormed and overcome with "brute physical strength."

Neither can be scaled or pierced with spiritual passion, with inflamed emotions.

We cannot force our way into the cloud of unknowing because we cannot conquer God.

We can only surrender.

It is a hard realization not only because we want to be judged by our strength and worthiness, but because of our spiritual expectations.

We thought as we started out that it would be, should be different. There would come a moment when the dark would give way to light, when the wall would give way to a transparent veil, when unknowing would give way to knowing. When, to be honest about it, faith would not be necessary, the veil of faith all but dissolved.

But it doesn't happen.

Not because we got it wrong, but because we got it right.

We have accepted the wall and learned to live with it. We have penetrated the cloud of unknowing, not with strength but with the power of love.

We have learned—if we have listened well—to love.

From Our Unknown Teacher

. . . to love with true fervor,
not with brute physical strength
and inflamed feelings,
but gently and peacefully
both in body and soul.

A Prayer of Unknowing

Here in the valley of desire
I am ringed round with walls of unknowing,
with walls that will never crumble,
with walls that cannot be stormed and overcome
with brute physical strength,
with the emotions
of an inflamed heart.
I cannot, I know, force my way
over or through a wall of unknowing
that stands between you and me.
I cannot conquer you,
but only surrender to your love,
gently and peacefully
in body and soul.
And let the walls stand.

24

Patience

Most of us can admit without embarrassment that we get impatient with ourselves. It's quite another thing to confess that we are impatient with God.

But the fact is that we want our spiritual journey to take place on our terms and most of all at our pace.

We are not content to wait "patiently, with courtesy and humility, on the will of the Lord"— confident that what needs to be done, the Lord will do. In her own good way. In her own good time.

That's the way it is has to be. And will be.

But that's not what we want to hear.

Because we are new at this, we want things to happen even when we are not sure of what we want. More to the point: we want to *make* them happen. And we want to make them happen *now*.

In our rush to get on our spiritual way we "snatch at life hurriedly, like a greedy animal."

Patience, with its insistence on courtesy and humility, goes against our grain. We are convinced that "it is only with brute physical strength, with obsessive will power, that we will capture the ear and heart of God."

Patience, we decide, is for the halfhearted, the spiritually weak-willed.

So we dismiss it without knowing what it is. And what it is not. Which is to make a crippling mistake. Patience is not lazy passivity. Not a pouting spirit. Not whining to the Lord.

It is not synonymous with "acquiescence" or a euphemism for biding our time quietly, often petulantly, until our expectations are met, until our hunger is satisfied. "Well, if I have to wait, I suppose I have to wait."

It is, rather, another name for the courage that it takes, the endurance that is demanded to choose and live a life in a land of desire, in a land of waiting and expectation.

It is the capacity to endure hardship, difficulty, and inconvenience without complaint. It is calmness, self-control, and the ability to tolerate delay. It is the capacity and willingness to bear suffering over a long period of time, courageously and without rancor.

It is about coping with everyday living. Nothing dramatic. Nothing unusual. Just life as it happens.

When theologians looked to locate it, they made it a child of fortitude.

Patience is a desert virtue whose synonym is *endurance.*

We are reminded that it is not so much, or only, that the valley of desire can be a harsh and unforgiving place, but that it is no place for cowards.

It is learning and accepting the fact that the characteristic virtues of our desert passage are not the silence and solitude that may have attracted us, but the quiet courage and patience that undergird them, that give them flesh, that stoke the endurance they demand.

Like it or not, our journey will be taken at God's pace.

It will mean learning to be patient, not just with ourselves but with the ways of God—which as often as not will not be our ways.

From Our Unknown Teacher

Wait patiently on the will of the Lord
with courtesy and humility
and not snatch at it hurriedly
like a greedy animal,
no matter how hungry we are.

A Prayer of Unknowing

Here in the valley of desire
I'll pretend for a moment
that I am patient,
that I live easily
with your ways.
But I am not patient,
not courageous.
I want it my way.
I want it now.
Understand, I beg you:
I am hungry
for what only you can give.
But let me not be mistaken.
It's you I want.
Help me do it your way.

25

Our Need to Know

It is hard to overestimate the comfort and the sense of security that comes with understanding. It brings with it a sense of power, of having control over our lives or at least some part of them, however small.

On the other hand, not to understand is to feel powerless. It is to experience the unease that comes when life seems beyond our control, the discomfort and insecurity of not knowing where we are. Not understanding is the feeling that we are lost.

We think of understanding as an anchor. Not to understand is to be adrift.

But understanding is not all that it claims to be. It makes promises that it cannot keep.

It leads us to believe that we can bypass the awful finitude of our existence, the fragility of our humanity, its radical unpredictability, its humbling incertitude. Its uncertainty.

But we can't.

We live in a shoreless sea of mystery of which we are a part. We cannot escape the continuity, the all-enveloping mystery in which we live and move and have our being.

In what matters most we do not understand, nor are we understandable. To others. To ourselves. Mystery does not begin at the cloud of unknowing's edge. It is *all* mysterious, *all* outside our power to capture and control. Our spiritual universe is unknowable *all* the way to and through the cloud of unknowing.

The incomprehensible is the world into which we were born, the world in which we live, the world that we must celebrate.

Therefore we will not really be able to reach out into the darkness of God, to puncture the cloud of unknowing until we welcome and celebrate its very darkness, its mystery, its unknowability—until we surrender our need to know.

To do otherwise is to undermine our spiritual journey before it can begin. In that moment when we settle for what is knowable, we settle for that which is not God. We settle for a clear image, which, however good, however beautiful, however God-like, is not God. There can be no clear image of that which cannot be imagined.

It is a price too great to pay for a moment or even a lifetime of comfort and security.

If we do not overcome our need to understand
It will undermine our quest.
It will replace the darkness
that we have pierced to reach God
with clear images of something
that however good, however beautiful,
however God-like
is not God.

Here in the valley of desire
I understand that
there is no way that I can bypass
the awful finitude of my existence,
the fragility of my humanity,
the radical unpredictability of my days,
my humbling incertitude,
my uncertainty.
There is no way.
But the truth is that I can recite
all the right words
and still be afraid of the dark,
still feel the need to understand,
still feel the need to control.
I'm only human.
I need to understand, to accept, this.

PART FOUR
GOD BEYOND GOD

The higher you ascend
the less you understand,
because the cloud
that lights up the night
is dark.
Whoever knows this
remains always in unknowing,
transcending all knowledge.

—John of the Cross

Tucked away at the center of hundreds of wooded acres, in the foothills of New Jersey's Kittatinny Mountains, there is a small, nameless lake at whose side I once lived for a year in a sustained, burden-free, ever growing, and ever more welcoming world of silence. And expectation.

I went there expecting to meet God—a God, that is, who at long last would speak to me clearly, whose presence would be palpable, whose face would emerge from the hills and the woods. A God who would offer me the certainty and security, the fresh start that I so deeply desired, a God in whose presence I could move beyond alienation and fear, beyond even an ordinary, decent life.

There, on warm August afternoons, I paddled a clunky little rowboat up and around the corner of the lake until I found even more of the quiet solitude I had come to lean on. There in the shallows, tied down a few feet from reedy shores, I could be alone in a world that felt safe, that felt spiritual—they were, after all, for me, pretty much the same thing. No one could see me from the porch, from the dam, from the swimming dock. I could read. I could say my prayers. I could foster dreams of God. And other dreams that I dared not name. I could hide. No one would know where I was, who I was, what I was thinking, what I was feeling. What I believed. What I didn't believe.

I listened with urgency. I strained to see. It was all very "spiritual."

It was all very secure.

And it was all very puzzling.

It would take me the better part of my lifetime to understand and accept the fact that a transformed life begins and continues not with the certainty and warm feelings that I harbored and trusted on those idyllic days, but with "desire," with longing, with wanting to go beyond where we are to become what we are meant to be.

It is, I have been frequently told, a matter of letting God have his way. It is surrendering to her mystery.

But in the quiet serenity of those summer afternoons, I could tell myself that more than anything else I wanted God and that in the summer stillness I had found the God I had come in search of.

I know now—and began to suspect, to know, even then—that what I really desired and what I found was only a shadow of God. What, in fact, I was looking for and prepared to settle for was peace and quiet, the serenity of untroubled days. The warm fuzziness of a first love, the enveloping laziness of the late afternoon sun.

And to call it God.

It was a case of mistaken identity.

In truth, what I wanted was not God but a shadow of God, a stand-in, a God born of my needs and tailored to my limitations. A God made in my own image and likeness.

I suppose I knew even then that the reality of God has little to do with quiet afternoons on mountain lakes—has little to do with serenity, comfort, and security.

I suppose I knew, even then, that to satisfy my God-hunger I would have to leave behind the comfortable and go to an unknown place, a place of unknowing, the deeper, more treacherous part of the lake. I knew I might drown there.

I would have to feel the earth shift beneath my certainties. I would have to let go of everything I had come to take for granted, everything I had mistaken for God.

I suppose I knew these things. But maybe not.

I suppose that deep down I knew I would have to decide whether it was God that I wanted or just his shadow. And to be willing to go wherever that decision would take me.

This much I did know—such a choice would not be easy. And it hasn't been.

On any given day what I experience might be God. But it could be nothing. But then again it could be God. I will never be sure. No one can be. We are the unknowing, and what is asked of us is not that we come to know, but that we accept our unknowing for what it is—a call to a life immersed in mystery.

It is the discomforting price we pay for leaving the shallows behind.

It is to understand and accept that what awaits us is not comforting arms, but a transcendent God, totally and unimaginably other—"a scalding vision," a friend has called it.

And we are permitted to wonder if we will ever love that God, whether we ever could, whether we will ever really believe that we are loved by that unknowable God—whether indeed this is God or just, in the words of the young Thomas Merton, a blind alley.

But there is something that I knew even then— there comes a time to stop running from the unknown. And the unknowable.

To stop denying the hunger of our heart.

To stop putting off our surrender to the mystery of God and begin to listen to the desires of our God-hungry heart.

"God will make you what he created you to be," Merton's friend Robert Lax once told him, "if you will consent to let him do it. All you have to do is desire it."

This is, however, not an easy lesson to learn, not an easy truth to accept.

In the years since those summer days, times without number, I have recognized what I was sure was God's knock, felt his approach, only to plead for time. I have hovered, played, I suppose, at the margins of a new life even as I settled for the careful "faith" that has been for as long as I can remember the air my soul has breathed. I have searched. Often. Everywhere. I have been reassured at one moment, only to be frightened and paralyzed the next.

The fact is that it has become over the years ever easier to be content with a kind of emptiness, a kind of half-life, a comfortable mix of personal history, formulas, celebrations, identity, security, and familiarity.

I have learned to protect my heart, careful not to get too close to the edge, careful not to let God get too close for comfort. I have always been able to find a word, a phrase, an argument, a formula to keep him at a distance and my heart safely in its comfort zone.

I have learned to protect myself with familiar words, to hide behind my prayer book. To convince myself that I need go no deeper, that this far is far enough, I have clung to whatever I could find to defuse the moment.

Again and again I have come close to giving in to her attraction, only to surrender a moment later to a paralyzing fear of the unknown and the unknowable. I have drifted into, even cultivated, a kind of spiritual complacency. It's easy to do. I have argued with myself that this is as good as I get, as good as I need to be, as close to God as I need to come. Anything more is more than I care to handle. It's much too scary. By any standards it is enough to be a "good person." It is enough to live an ordinary, decent life.

But I have long known that this is not what I want. This is not what I hunger for. Not by a long shot.

I hunger for a life beyond the quiet waters, beyond the shallows.

Beyond comfort. Beyond knowing.

Beyond the quiet serenity of a mountain lake.

Beyond an ordinary, decent life.

I want to surrender to the God who has never ceased to pull at my soul, who never will—the God in whose embrace I can at last become fully human, fully the person I was meant to be, the person I want to be.

I don't expect instant fulfillment or a sense of completion. I expect to go on living with uncertainty and unknowing because nothing more is possible. The spirituality of unknowing, to repeat myself, will always be a spirituality of discontent, of desire, of restlessness, of longing for something better, for something more. And to repeat what the Canadian reviewer wrote of Thomas Merton: "we will almost certainly live out our lives without ever experiencing a sense of having it all together."

But it will be enough to know that there is a God. To know that there is no God. To know, in the words of the theologian, that there is God beyond God.

A Prayer of Unknowing

Here in the valley of desire
my heart is uneasy.
I am not yet where I want to be.
I am not yet who I want to be.
I am still not sure where I want to go.
I am immersed in mystery,
in your mystery,

in what I do not, cannot know.
I need to trust you.
But trust does not come easily to me.
I am more afraid than I can say.
But I need to trust you.
I need—must—
put my life in your hands,
even though
there is a part of me
that will not surrender,
that thinks there must be more to it than this.
But there isn't.
Just this terrible simplicity.
This frightening clarity.
This need to trust you
with my life.
Be there, I beg you
to catch me
when I let go.

—*Lakeside,* August 2002

The classic spirituality of the centuries-old The Cloud of Unknowing *is alive and well in the widespread centering prayer movement that has developed in our times.*

Inspired by the Trappist monk Fr. Thomas Keating, it is a simple and profound three-step program available to anyone who, in the spirit of The Cloud of Unknowing, *is willing to spend twenty minutes each day immersed in the mystery of God, their intellect set aside, their will ready to go where only love can lead them.*

For more information, you may wish to contact Contemplative Outreach Ltd., 9 William Street, P.O. Box 737, Butler, NJ 07403, (201) 838-3384, www.contemplativeoutreach.org

The author may be reached
at john@johnkirvan.com
His website is
JohnKirvan.com

A group discussion guide
designed especially for study groups
is available for downloading at
sorinbooks.com

Recommended Reading

Open Mind, Open Heart, Thomas Keating, O.C.S.O. (Continuum). (The basic text of the Centering Prayer movement).

The series *Thirty Days With a Great Spiritual Teacher* (Ave Maria Press), especially:

Where Only Love Can Go: A Journey of the Soul Into "The Cloud of Unknowing," John Kirvan (Ave Maria Press).

Fear Not the Night: Based on the Classic Spirituality of John of the Cross, John Kirvan (Ave Maria Press).

The Cloud of Unknowing, The Classics of Western Spirituality (Paulist Press).

The Mysticism of "The Cloud of Unknowing," William Johnston (Fordham University Press).

JOHN KIRVAN is the author of three companion books on the inner life: *God Hunger: Discovering the Mystic in All of Us*, *Raw Faith: Nurturing the Believer in All of Us*, and *Silent Hope: Living With the Mystery of God*. He is also the author of the highly successful *Thirty Days With a Great Spiritual Teacher* series, a library of fourteen books that offer the wisdom of the mystics for daily meditation. He currently lives in Southern California, where he writes primarily about classical spirituality.